BARKING UP THE WRONG TREE
ESCAPING THE RELIGIOUS LIE OF DO TO BECOME

DON KEATHLEY

THE WRITER'S SOCIETY | A GRASSROOTS PUBLISHING COMPANY

Copyright © 2022 by Don Keathley

All rights reserved.

No part of this book may be reproduced in any form or by any electronic or mechanical means, including information storage and retrieval systems, without written permission from the author, except for the use of brief quotations in a book review.

Unhook the Book was published by The Writer's Society a grace based Trinitarian grassroots publishing company empowering authors to release books that reveal God's goodness to the world through a variety of self publishing services.

www.thewriterssociety.online

CONTENTS

Introduction	v
1. Two Trees	1
2. The Branches	9
3. Moving From Law To Grace	22
4. Branch of Trust - Part 1	30
5. Branch of Trust - Part two	40
6. Branch of Love	54
Other Books By Don Keathley	69
NOTES	71
NOTES	73
NOTES	75
NOTES	76
NOTES	77

INTRODUCTION

Have you ever heard the expression, barking up the wrong tree? In this book, we'll look at two trees and their branches to see if we are barking up the wrong one or tapping into the right one. Perhaps you've wondered what these two trees are all about? How they affect you and impact how you live your daily life today? And this book might bring a unique spin and different insight than you've been taught.

The tree of the knowledge of good and evil puts its money on your performance through knowledge. Learning what you do to earn from God and become like God. However, the tree of life develops trust in what He has done, confidence in His performance, and puts absolutely zero faith in your performance.

Paul and Jesus lived this out. What did it look like in the life of Jesus? Here is how He expressed living from the tree of life as opposed to living from the tree of the intellect, known as the tree of the knowledge of good and evil. For example, in John 5:30, Jesus said, *"I can of My own self do nothing."* Can you honestly say that? Or do you think that the only time God comes through is when you've done all you can do, and then He makes up the difference? It doesn't work that way. When you eat from the tree of life, you then like, Jesus can say, "of myself, I can do nothing." Jesus said, *"As I hear, I judge; and My judgment is righteous, because I do not seek My own will, but the will of the Father who sent Me."* And look at what He says in John 5:19, *Jesus answered and said to them, "Most assuredly, I say to you, the Son can do nothing of Himself. But what He sees the Father do, for whatever the Father does, the Son also does in like manner."* That's eating from the tree of life. Jesus made no dependence upon what He knew, His abilities, His thoughts, or what He could achieve.

Whatever the Father does, the Son does. The Son mimics it. He does the same. And He says this over and over and over. Expressing to us what it looks like living out of the tree of life. In John 8:28 (NKJV), *Jesus said to them, "When you lift up the Son of Man, then you will know that I am He and that I do nothing of Myself. But as My Father taught Me, I speak these things."* What's Jesus saying here? He's saying I'm not connected to anything but the source of life. Everything I do flows from the one source of what the Father does. And Paul said in Galatians 2:20 that he had been crucified with Christ. And it was no longer him **doing to be**. He was living from the Tree of Life within. He said it is Christ who lives in him. That was the life source of his life, the Christ within.

So, we see in the life of Jesus and Paul, they made no independent determinations apart from the Father. They fed on life itself. And as they fed on life itself, life decisions were made. That means that you must decrease, and He must increase, until finally, you can say, it's no longer I who live, it's Christ that lives in me. Getting to the place where we are no longer trusting in our own ability but trusting in His ability. And to trust His ability, the trust in our ability must diminish.

The Christ in every man is the Tree of Life and floods our hearts with revelation. And as His revelation floods our hearts, our minds are challenged to repent, to change, and move in another direction. To be renewed to what the Source of life is feeding it. It challenges it to trust and love. And our actions and choices change. Because our minds have chosen to submit to the revelation from the Christ within instead of relying on our knowledge of good and evil. We're being fed by the Source of life instead of what we must **do to become**. And suddenly, Scriptures like Philippians 2:13 make a lot of sense. *It is God who works in you, both to will and to do of His good pleasure.*

When you stop depending on yourself and start trusting Him. And you get rid of your **doing to become**, and tap into His love, suddenly you see that it's God who works in you. He's not working in your head. He's working in your spirit. And He's working on two things in your life. He's working His will in your spirit, and He's working the ability to do that will. Because it's God, who works in us both to will and to do His good pleasure. Do you want to do God's pleasure? Let Him work the will and the doing. We are always trying to work the will and the doing. But it's the tree of life that births the will of God. Just like it did in the garden. And it gives us everything necessary to do what His will for us is. The will of God in the garden was just to keep it, dress it, and take care of it. And He gave them everything necessary to do that.

> **When God drops His will for you into His life, He will give you everything you need. He will provide you with the ability to do His will.**

Let's respond to the stir of the Holy Spirit and let go of the wrong tree. Let's embrace the right tree, the tree of life. If you're making business decisions, buying a house, raising your kids, taking a job, or moving to another state, which tree are you feeding from? Are you feeding from the tree of life? You are if you are responding and following the Holy Spirit's initial prompting in your spirit.

Be sensitive. Hear what's going on in your spirit. Stop passing everything through filters in your head. You may miss it sometimes. This is something you work at. This is not something that you hit 100%. But I know from experience that the more you stop trusting yourself and start trusting Him in everything, the stronger and more reliable it becomes. So, the next time you see a person on the corner holding up a sign, listen in your spirit to whether you should give them money? Don't sit there sizing him up and reasoning to yourself, well, *you know, he doesn't look all that needy to me. I'm gonna pass this one by.* Or thinking, *my heart goes out to this poor guy. Look at him.* No. Listen in your spirit. The tree of life in your spirit will guide you in everything. He will tell you all things. Remember, God works in you both to will and do of His good pleasure.

As you read this book, light will come on regarding these two trees, causing you to see you've been eating from the tree of the knowledge of good and evil. You've been setting the tree of life aside. But the Holy Spirit, through grace, is restoring awareness of our correct identity, removing fear, and focusing us on what we need to focus on. He's weaning us from our ability to think from the knowledge of good and evil and **do to become**. He's saying, "Look, you've already got the garden of Eden. You don't have to do to become. You've got everything you need. Now simply enjoy it. Look at all I've given you."

Let's live out of the source of Life within, the Tree of Life.

1
TWO TREES

Genesis 2:9 says, *and out of the ground, the Lord God made every tree grow that is pleasant to the sight and good for food. The tree of life was also in the midst of the garden, and the tree of the knowledge of good and evil.* So, we see God planted all the trees in the garden. And it mentions two of the trees by name. One is called the tree of the knowledge of good and evil. The other is called the tree of life.

In Genesis 2, God places man in the garden of Eden, where He had planted the two trees. Verses 15-17 say, *Then the Lord God took the man and put him in the garden of Eden to tend and keep it. [16] And the Lord God commanded the man, saying, "Of every tree of the garden you may freely eat; [17] but of the tree of the knowledge of good and evil you shall not eat, for in the day that you eat of it you shall surely die."* God puts these two trees of notoriety in the garden and tells man not to eat from the one. But of the other tree, He told him to eat from it to his heart's content. He told him, "Don't eat from the tree that gives you the knowledge of good and evil, but of the tree of life. It's all yours."

. . .

These two trees still grow in the hearts of men today. Each tree produces different fruit. And there are two main branches that grow out of them. But before I talk to you about these branches that grow out of those trees, let's define these two trees. The tree of knowledge of good and evil speaks to the totality of man having knowledge of all things. It's goal is man being omniscient. Becoming all-knowing, having all knowledge, and living out of that understanding. Its aim is to make us gods by omniscience, by knowing everything apart or independent from God.

The term good and evil is called a merism. A merism combines two contrasting words that refer to an entirety. The merism of Genesis 2 refers to the totality of knowledge between good and evil. They are found throughout Scripture. For example, in Genesis 1:1, *God created the heavens and the earth.* The heavens and the earth are separate terms. They are a merism. God not only created the heavens and the earth. He made everything that exists between them. Another merism is that God knows the end from the beginning. Knowing the end from the beginning, He knows their entirety. He knows everything contained within them. We also find these contrasts in life. When you married, the minister used the phrases such as, for better or worse, and for richer or poorer. A merism is an entirety that exists between those terms. It refers to everything between richer and poorer, and better and worse.

The serpent comes to Eve and says, if you eat of the tree of the knowledge of good and evil, you will be like God. The assumption is that once you eat from the tree of the knowledge of good and evil, you will know all things in their entirety. Wisdom will come to you, and you can become the god of your own life. You will be omniscient, knowing all things independent from God. The enemy says to Eve, through this merism, once you tap into the knowledge of good and evil, it will cover the entire street of knowledge. You will know all things.

The more fruit you pick and eat from one tree, the more enormous and robust that tree and its branches become.

Two branches grow out of each of these trees. The two branches of performance and fear grow from the tree of the knowledge of good and evil. The idea is that the more you know, the better you can perform in life. And fear comes from failing to do well enough. Which is inevitable. And religion has done an excellent job of fertilizing that tree to grow big, strong, healthy branches of performance and fear. Religion was born in the garden. It taught that knowledge is king. The more you learn, the more knowledge you have. The more you can be, the more you can become. The essence of religion is training man to choose the good and not the evil. Religion eats from the tree of the knowledge of good to gain all knowledge.

An example from the old covenant is Deuteronomy chapter 30, verse 19 (NKJV) *I call heaven and earth to witness today against you that I have set before you life and death, blessing and cursing.* The law is about attempting to live out of the tree of the knowledge of good and evil. Notice the merisms in this verse. The choice is between good and not evil. It is choosing life and not death. Choosing the blessing and not the cursing. There's a duality that's working here. But God doesn't give them a duality to choose from. What does He give them? "I've set before you life and death, blessing and cursing."

. . .

He doesn't want us to choose between them. He wants us to stay out of that duality mode of thinking. There is only one choice, LIFE. And out of that tree comes all you need. God doesn't want us to make determinations. And I know we're very accustomed to learning how to pick the good over the evil or choosing right over wrong. Much of what we've learned in churches programmed us and groomed us to respond and act that way. In this book, I'll show you how to stop barking up the wrong tree and return to the tree we should eat from without limits. The tree of life.

There are absolute distinctions between the two trees. And you'll see how you've been eating from the wrong tree under the guise of religion. And we have become comfortable using it to make decisions in life. But the only tree we want to eat from is the tree of life. According to several sources, including research by Roberts Wesleyan College, the average adult makes about 35,000 decisions a day. That's astounding, isn't it? 35,000 decisions a day on everything. We all know we make many choices and decisions, but I never thought it would be that much. But then I started watching how choosing one thing is not picking something else. It can add up. We all decide about marriage, raising kids, jobs, personal relationships, how we will spend our time, etc. And whether we realize it or not, every decision we make, or most of the decisions we are conscious of, we eat from one of two trees planted in our hearts. Either from the tree of the knowledge of good and evil, or the tree of life.

For most of us, the tree of the knowledge of good and evil is our go-to tree. Why? Because we've been trained to eat from that tree. Our culture, school, church, etc., taught us to make choices based on our knowledge. You know the old sayings that knowledge is power, and knowledge is king. The tree of the knowledge of good and evil's main aim is to teach us: **do to become.** Adam and Eve were told they would become like God if they did something. There's always some kind of performance attached to the **do to be** which comes from the tree of the knowledge of good and evil. We were taught in church that salvation comes from what we do. Becoming a child of God and becoming like Jesus results from our actions. The tree of the knowledge of good and evil is the tree that enforces the idea that we are self-determining people. And that the choices and decisions we make reign supreme in life. And because knowledge is king and power, we work hard to accumulate knowledge. The goal is to learn as much as possible. So, at some level, we get as close to becoming omniscient as God. We often think that if we can get enough knowledge and information, we can make the right choices in life. And by attaining the correct knowledge, we can do good and not evil and eliminate poor decisions and choices.

Generations of religion have taught Scripture from the knowledge of good and evil. We all have come through these religious systems, which use lots of misunderstood and misinterpreted "proof text" Scriptures to back up their teaching. It was the knowledge of good and evil. The knowledge that would help us: **do to become**. Learning what we need to do to live the abundant life that Jesus said He came to give us. We've tied many of our ideas around our ability to gain spiritual knowledge by reading the word, digesting it, and meditating on it to fill ourselves full of it. Hearing teachings and messages geared toward training us what is good and evil. Teaching us what is right and wrong.

Jesus stated in John 5:39 (NKJV), *"You search the Scriptures for in them you think you have eternal life, and these are they which testify of Me."*

The point of Scripture is that it should point to Jesus. When we read or study Scripture, the primary thrust should be to point us to Jesus. Jesus told them in John 5 that they weren't searching the Scriptures to point them to Him. They thought by learning enough Scriptures, they could have eternal life. But He said, *"The truth is they are those which testify of Me."* Then he said in verse 40 (NKJV), *"But you're not willing to come to Me that you might have life."* Jesus is drawing a contrast here. He's saying there's a right and a wrong way to find eternal life. The wrong way is by thinking that we find it through the Scriptures. He said the only way you find life is by coming to Me. Are you with me so far?

Jesus distinguishes between trying to find life in Scripture and coming to Him. He's contrasting the trees: seeking life through the tree of the knowledge of good and evil, doing to become, versus coming to Him, the Tree of Life, so that you can find life. Jesus says often we are heading in the wrong direction. And I think it would be a fair assumption to say that we have made the Bible into the tree of the knowledge of good and evil. We've used our bibles to search out what is good, what is evil, what is right, and what is wrong. And we've hoped that if we could somehow get enough Bible verses in us, we could find life. The Bible contains words about God, but it is not the totality of the Word of God. And what we've done is that we've elevated gaining knowledge of the Bible, thinking that if we can get enough knowledge from it, we would become like God. I don't want to shock you too much. But the Bible is not the 4th person of the Godhead. Now listen, I'm not putting Scripture down. I want to elevate Jesus to the position He needs to be in. I want to lift Him up.

There are two trees we can choose to eat from looking for life. One is the tree of the knowledge of good and evil. But Jesus said that's not the tree where you will find life. He said you must go to the Tree of Life to find life.

There is a lot of discussion today about the inerrancy of the word. Is the word of God inerrant? Only one version of the word is inerrant. The version of the Word that became flesh and dwelt among us, and we beheld His glory as the only Son of God. His name is Jesus. Now, folks, I love my Bible; you know that. I use lots of Scriptures when I teach. I read it every day. In fact, I cannot tell you the last time I didn't read something in the Bible. I study it.

But Jesus makes this astounding statement in verse 40 of John chapter five. And it gets me thinking that He's talking to people who are continually in the Scriptures. They are constantly in the word of God. But they're missing the life that Jesus came to give. Because they're looking at Scripture to provide them with life through the knowledge of good and evil. And Jesus said that's not where you're gonna find life. He said, "You find life when you come to Me." There is only one source of life, and it's not the B I B L E. The one and only source of life is J E S U S. There is one source of life, and it's not King James. It's King Jesus. He alone is the source of life.

In John 6:63, Jesus says, *"It is the Spirit who gives life, the flesh profits nothing. The words I speak to you, they are spirit, and they are life."* The words Jesus speaks to us are not the knowledge of good and evil or right and wrong. They are words of life from the tree of life. Jesus encourages us to eat from this tree all day long. The only tree God said to stay away from was the tree of the knowledge of good and evil. It brings us duality: good and evil, right and wrong. It teaches us about a greater power overcoming a lesser power. There is only one source of all things. There is one power and one knowledge. The tree of life is the one source that entirely depends on God's omniscience to lead us. The Tree of Life sees no duality. Therefore, it brings no duality to the scene. It brings us no knowledge of good and evil, of right and wrong. It just brings us the one Source of all to draw wisdom and understanding from the Father.

The deception that comes from eating from this tree is that we can learn to grow in knowledge independent of God. I've done it in my life. For years and years, I made the Bible into the tree of the knowledge of good and evil. It trained me and convinced me that my will supersedes His will. How? By applying what I know, what I decide, and what I think. One of the heresies in the early church was Gnosticism. And it still runs strong today. Gnosticism's most simplistic definition says true freedom comes through superior knowledge. And if we were truthful this morning as believers, we'll admit that the flux of our time has been spent trying to gain knowledge. Trying to gain understanding.

The tree of the knowledge of good and evil works in your head. But the Tree of Life flows through your spirit.

2

THE BRANCHES

This tree of life that we are to eat from, that we're tuned into, has two great branches that grow out of it. One branch is called trust. And the trust branch increases our trust and dependence on Him while decreasing our trust and reliance on self. When you eat from the tree of life, you develop trust and lean into Him because you don't have to figure everything out and make everything click yourself. The tree of the knowledge of good and evil convinces us that if we can get enough knowledge, the responsibility for making things work lies within our own abilities and power.

But when you eat from the tree of life, there is the assurance that you can trust Him. And that trust lets you rest. The trust developed in Him by eating from the tree of life releases our death grip on a life that creates stress, anxiety, turmoil, and tension because we're now abandoning control. However, the tree of the knowledge of good and evil teaches us to be in control. Teaching that if we just gain more knowledge, we will make the right decisions and choices, and life will go well. And you get under this burden where you feel you must perform; you are responsible for making it all come together. And if it's not coming together, then it's because you don't know enough.

But when you eat from the tree of life, you rest in Him. And as you rest in Him, you understand that He's the only One responsible for making it all work. He's the One responsible for bringing it together. But the tree of the knowledge of good and evil puts you in control. You call the shots, and your will is supreme. While the Tree of Life simply allows you to enter the unforced rhythms of grace. And you flow in His life and wisdom. There's an unbelievable difference between gaining knowledge so that you will be in control and just entering His grace and flowing in His life.

This tree of the knowledge of good and evil teaches us how to perform. The fundamental basis of religion is: **do to become**. You are the initiator. You do the doing, and then God responds to your doing.

So, when the serpent comes to Eve, He says if you just perform, if you just **do to become** like God, you can get closer to God. And usually, those kinds of choices come from a sincere heart. Because we want to be more like God, right? We want more godliness in our life. And so, we look to make good choices.

In Genesis 3:5, we see the dialogue between the serpent and Eve. And the serpent says, *"For God knows that the day you eat of it, your eyes will be opened, and you will be like God, knowing everything, knowing good and evil."* He uses a merism. He says, "In the day you eat of it, you will know good, evil, and everything in between." What is he saying? This tree would give them all knowledge. The temptation of the tree was to gain knowledge, making them more like God. It sounds good, right? I mean, who doesn't want to become more like God? Who doesn't want to achieve godliness? It sounds like a worthy ambition. And so, the serpent comes in and says, "If you just do, you will be."

When you look back over your life, how many things were you taught that if you would just do, you would be? For example, if you just do such and such, you will grow spiritually. Or if you just do this or that, God will be pleased with you. And salvation and blessings come from you doing this or that.

Watch how this branch of fear grows after they eat from this tree of **doing to become**. Eve bites the fruit, and then she gives it to her husband. Genesis 3:6, *when the woman saw the tree was good for food, that it was pleasant to the eyes, and a tree desirable to make one wise, she took off its fruit and ate. She also gave to her husband with her, and he ate it*. What a big dummy standing there with her watching the whole thing. We think Adam was off somewhere else, and Eve found him and made a deceptive move to get him to eat the fruit. No. He was standing there watching his wife go through all this, and he didn't tell the devil, the serpent, "Look, guy, why don't you just bug off? We're not interested." Nope, that didn't happen. Instead, he's standing there with her, and he ate it.

Then verse seven says, *Then the eyes of both of them were opened, and they knew that they were naked*. So now they are getting this good and evil knowledge. And verses 7b-10, *And they sewed fig leaves together and made themselves coverings. [8] And they heard the sound of the LORD God walking in the garden in the cool of the day, and Adam and his wife hid themselves from the presence of the Lord among the trees of the garden. [9] Then the Lord called to Adam and said to him, where are you? [10] So he said, I heard your voice in the garden; I was afraid because I was naked. And I hid myself.*

Now, isn't it amazing that their performance didn't deliver what the DO promised to deliver? And I found that many times in religion, we do the doing, but the DO doesn't deliver on what it promised. Because the truth is our performance never gets us where it promises, it always falls short. And we can see in this garden story that when their do falls short, as it always does, verse 10 tells us that fear entered. And along with fear, a feeling of separation from God. When religion chides us to do to become, and we do it, our performance always falls short. Why? Because there's always been something more to do. Fear enters because we failed and fell short of the DO. And with that fear because of failing comes the sense of being separated from God. And so, what do we do? We double down on the doing. Feeling that we need to do more because the first doing failed. So, we **do to become** again. But it never takes us where it promises it will take us. And we end up more fearful of God, and with that fear is a greater sense of separation in our minds. All because we thought God wanted us to do more to become like Him.

Fear and separation create a false sense of identity. And we see ourselves in the wrong light, in a diminished light. And this is where many people are. They see themselves in an entirely false light, in a distorted image, thinking this is also how God sees them. Why? Because they don't feel they have done what they need to do to make themselves acceptable and satisfactory to God. And the natural feeling, because they think they have failed God, is to fear Him. That's what happened to Adam and Eve. They feared God and felt a sense of separation because they failed Him.

. . .

What is the biggest fear of religion? What does religion threaten people with if they don't **do to become**? If you don't pray the prayer to be saved what happens? What is the fear religion attaches to that? Eternal separation from God. The branches of performance and fear will always grow the fruit of separation, producing more fear. And the religious formulas we've got to **do to become** are wide and varied. But every religious **do to become** formula carries two characteristics within it. The first characteristic is that the responsibility lies with us to do the doing. And the second is that separation is our eternal future if we fall short of doing what is right.

But the question is: does man have to do to become?

Because that's what religion has drilled into us all our life in church. You must do the right things to be. And so, we come to church every week, and what we hear is a message on **do to become**. However, do we have to **do to become**? Is that how God designed our lives to be? That's the lie Adam and Eve fell for. Convinced they had to **do something to become** like God. When in reality, they were already like God. Created in His image and likeness. But in most churches, you'll often hear a message trying to convince you what you need to **do to become** who you already are.

Let's just walk through a couple scriptures. And let's start with the creation of mankind.

> Genesis 1:26 (NKJV), *then God said, "Let Us make man in Our image, according to Our likeness, and let them have dominion over the fish of the sea, over the birds of the air, and over the cattle, over the earth, and over every creeping thing that creeps on the earth."*

What did you do to become in God's image and likeness? What did you do to get it? Nothing. Why? Because that's what God created you to be. He said, let Us make man in Our image and likeness. So, when you sit under teaching or go to a church that's teaching you to **do to become** more like God, you need to ask yourself how can you become more godly than image and likeness of God? Instead, you should learn how to push off all the religious rubble and mess so that you can realize your identity and stop trying to become who God says you already are. Simply understanding who He created you already to be. There was no **doing to become** in God's image and likeness. You didn't earn it. He gave it.

Let me walk you through another one.

> 2 Corinthians 5:21(NKJV) says, *for He made Him who knew no sin to be sin for us, that we might become the righteousness of God in Him.*

Look at what a great exchange that is. Jesus took your sin and gave you, His righteousness. He made Him who knew no sin to be sin for us so that we who knew no righteousness were made the righteousness of God in Christ. So, what did you **do to become** the righteousness of God in Christ? Was there anything you had to **do to become**? Was there any stipulation or footnotes of your Bible that say you must pray the sinner's prayer or live a particular lifestyle? Are there any conditions in your Bible for you to go to one specific church, believe a particular doctrine, or hang with a specific group of people? Was there any stipulation He placed on your becoming righteous? Was there any doing required on your part? No. Being made in His image and likeness and becoming the righteousness of God in Christ is all His doing. It is what He has imparted to us apart from anything we do.

Let's look at another one, and this one is so good.

Titus 3:4 (NKJV) says, *but when the kindness and love of God, our Savior toward man appeared.*

When God's love and kindness towards you appears, it will change your life. Once you see it and grasp it, things happen suddenly. And it all happens apart from your doing. If we could just get God's people to stop trying to do and realize who they are. That they don't have to **do to become.** So, it says, the kindness and love of God appeared. It was revealed to you. You see it. You grasp it. It's grounded in you. Now watch what happens.

Paul tells us in verse five that the kindness and love of God, our Savior, that appeared toward us did not come from a work of righteousness that we have done. But it came according to His mercy. He saved us. It didn't happen by works of righteousness. It was all His doing.

If you want to make a note in your Bible, a work of righteousness is anything you can do to make yourself right with God. Anything.

If you and I were to sit across the table at Starbucks, having a cup of coffee, and I were to say to you, what do you think made you right with God? And you say, "Well, I prayed the prayer. I signed the card. I'm faithful in going to church." That's works of righteousness. Anything apart from resting in what He's done is **doing to become**. That's a work of righteousness. Paul said it was according to His mercy, not giving us what we deserved. He saved us. How? The last part of verse 5 says, *through the washing of regeneration and renewing of the Holy Spirit*. And verse 6 says, *Whom He poured out on us abundantly through Jesus Christ our Savior.*

So, what did you do to get His mercy? What did you do for the washing of regeneration and renewing of the Holy Spirit? How did you get all this? Verse 6 says *He poured it out abundantly through Jesus Christ, our Savior.* And verse 7 says, *Having been justified by His grace, that we should become heirs according to the hope of eternal life.* Did you do anything to be justified? No. Our justification came solely by His grace. There is nothing you need to **do to become** more justified than you already are. Can you just become settled on that for all time in your life? There's no work of righteousness that you can do to make yourself right with God.

But how about this separation thing? Two branches grow out of the tree of the knowledge of good and evil. One is the performance which you must do to become. And we just walked through a few Scriptures that neutralize everything you thought you had to do to be made right with God. We've established that it has nothing to do with your performance. That can be difficult to grasp because we've been so well-schooled in our performance to be right with God.

. . .

And the other branch is fear. So, let me ask you a second question: is separation from God a legitimate fear? Is there any time you should fear being separated from God? We've just seen there is nothing we must do to become righteous. We can get rid of that in our thinking. But should we ever fear separation from God?

Let's go back to Genesis when Adam first messed up. Genesis 3:8 (NKJV) says, *they heard the sound of the LORD God walking in the garden of the cool of the day, and Adam and his wife hid themselves from the presence of the Lord.* In my Bible, I underlined the words they hid themselves from the presence of the Lord. Why? Because anytime you're not in the presence of the Lord, it's because you've hidden from God. It's not because He hasn't come to you. It says they hid from the Lord's presence among the garden trees. Then the Lord God called to Adam and said to him, "Where are you?" (verse 9). As if God didn't know where they were! This sense of separation was in the mind of Adam. It was Adams doing, not God's. God went looking for Adam. He made His presence known to Adam.

Separation from God was not a legitimate feeling that Adam had to carry. It was one he created for himself by his actions. When his **doing to become** like God failed, it brought fear to his life. Fear that God would now be angry with him because he didn't measure up, his doing fell short. And because of that fear, he hid and thought he was separated from God. And I see this often in people's lives when they feel like they have failed God. When they believe they have yet to measure up by what they do. It causes a fear of God because they think they're unworthy in His sight. And when we feel unworthy and fearful of God, we create a feeling of separation within ourselves. It never comes from God. He always comes looking for you. And He always surrounds you with His presence.

. . .

Colossians chapter 1 addresses whether separation from God is a legitimate fear. Verse 19-20 says, *for it pleased the Father that in Him [Jesus] all the fullness should dwell, and by Him to reconcile all things to Himself, whether things on earth or things in heaven, having made peace through the blood of His cross.* All things. Things on earth and things in heaven. Paul's using a merism again. Things on earth AND things in heaven. So, if He reconciled everything in heaven and on earth to Himself, there was nothing that wasn't reconciled. Are you with me? Verse 21 says, *and you who were once alienated and enemies in your minds by wicked works, yet now He has reconciled.*

Is this fear of separation legitimate? Absolutely not.

The only time you were ever alienated from God was when you did something that alienated God from you in your mind. He always comes looking. God always reconciles. God always restores. His presence is never far from us. It always surrounds us. Romans 8 tells us that nothing can separate us from the love of God. It says there is no height, depth, principality, etc., that can separate us from the love of God. Nothing. Separation from God is never a legitimate feeling.

God, knowing that Adam and Eve had sinned, refused to separate Himself from them. The fear, the separation, and the guilt over their failed performance alienated God in Adams's mind. But when God looked at Adam, He didn't see a broken relationship. Nor did He see broken fellowship. He did not separate Himself from Adam. And yet this whole scenario of God separating Himself from Adam and subsequently from fallen man is being played out worldwide. And almost every church today preaches a message about performance or **doing to become** what we already are. People hear then that if they don't perform, God will not be pleased. This opens the door to fear. And when they inevitably fail in their performance, this sense of separation sets in. And they feel alienated from God. But the whole thing is a deception.

In Jesus and Paul's life, we see how to cut the limbs of performance and fear off that tree and get the tree of life flourishing. How did they do that? How did they uproot the tree of the knowledge of good and evil? And how could they get the Tree of Life to flourish in their life? They both did it by showing us our authentic identity, image, and likeness of God. They both did it by exposing this lie of separation. And they both did it by driving out all fear with perfect love. That's what grace does. Grace reveals your true identity. It exposes the lie of separation. And when perfect love comes in, every fear you've had of being separated and alienated is driven out.

But the problem is religion refuses to acknowledge this. And they continue eating from the tree of the knowledge of good and evil. And those branches of performance and fear continue to grow strong.

What we're doing today is simply awakening to the Tree of Life's knowledge and understanding. It's awakening to His wisdom and understanding. It's seeing that this is God's initiative. He's revealing His life in us. He's waking us up to the Tree of Life in us. This tree has two branches. Trust and love. And the more you eat from the tree of life, the more you trust Him.

Proverbs 3 says, *Trust in the Lord, with all your heart, not your head. It says, do not lean to your own understanding.* What does understanding mean? That's your mind. The tree of the knowledge of good and evil dwells in your head. Refrain from leaning to the understanding of the knowledge of good and evil. Stop thinking that more knowledge and understanding will lead to a better life. He said don't lean to that, but acknowledge Him in all your ways, and He will direct your path. And then trust in God and diminishing reliance on yourself begin to grow. Whereas the tree of the knowledge of good and evil wants you to trust yourself. To trust your knowledge, understanding, ability, choices, and wisdom. The tree of life pulls that lie out by the roots. It says there's only One you can trust, the Tree of Life. Lean, not to your own understanding. Trust in the Lord with all your heart; He will direct your path. And as this branch strengthens, you'll depend less on your ability and more on His ability. You'll trust more in His insight and less in your insight. You'll realize the futility of trying to do it your way and understand the wisdom of doing it His way.

The second branch is the branch of love. As you eat from the Tree of Life, His branch of love assures you that He is pleased with you, just as you are. And you understand that your performance, choices, and decisions have zero to do with who you are. The tree of the knowledge of good and evil causes you to develop an identity of who you are based on your performance of doing good and shunning evil. But when you eat from the tree of life, you understand that your identity is not based on what you do. It's based on who He made you be apart from what you do.

Paul prays for the church in Ephesus, and he says in chapter 3, verse 17 (NKJV), *I pray that Christ would dwell in your hearts through faith and that you'd be rooted and grounded in love.* And then he says in verse 18 that when they're rooted and grounded in love, they can comprehend the width, length, depth, and height of that love with all the saints. Here Paul uses a merism when talking about the love of God.

He says width and length, depth, and height. In other words, we can comprehend the absolute love of God. Understanding everything in the width, length, depth, and height of God's love. And in verse 19, he says, *and to know the love of Christ, which passes knowledge.* You cannot conceive in your mind the depth, the height, the breadth, the width of the love God has for you. The tree of knowledge of good and evil cannot comprehend that. You can only understand it through the tree of life.

Paul says, "Don't go the knowledge route. This love of Christ goes beyond knowledge. It goes beyond what you get from the tree of the knowledge of good and evil." You may spend all your life trying to accumulate knowledge. Thinking it enables you to do more or better. But you inevitably will fall short. And when you fall short, it creates fear in your life. Fear that says you have failed God. And when you believe you failed God, you feel separated from Him. But Paul says, "You can eliminate that whole mess by letting this branch of love grow strong in your life. And you are filled with all the fullness of God as you grasp the height, depth, width, and length and know the love of Christ, which passes all understanding.

As the tree of life grows, the branches of trust and love grow more robust and have lots of fruit hanging off their limbs.

3
MOVING FROM LAW TO GRACE

One Sunday after church, a person I respect and appreciate a lot said something that could have offended me. But it didn't. Why? Because it's hard to be offended when somebody tells you the truth. They said, "Pastor, it seems like 40 to 50% of what you say to us is *'you've always been taught, or you've always heard,'* and then you tell us something contrary to what we've always been taught." And I thought about that, and it's probably true. But as I read the Sermon on the Mount in Matthew, I looked at Jesus. In Matthew chapter five, verses 21,27,33,38 and 43, Jesus said, *"You have heard it said."* And then every time in the next verse, He said, *"But I say unto you."* And what Jesus said unto them was contrary to what they had always been taught.

Now, there's a reason Jesus did that. And maybe I subconsciously do it for the same reason. The reason Jesus did that is He was always trying to move them from law to grace, from the tree of the knowledge of good and evil to the tree of life. So, He would quote the Scripture that they had always been taught, and then He would phrase it and couch it in a way to raise the level of the law to a standard they could not reach. Why? To make them dependent on God's grace, realizing they could not do what the law required. For example, He said, "You've always heard it said you should love people that do good to you, and you can destroy your enemies. But I say you should love your enemies." Did you catch what He did there? That was a very subtle law He was putting in there, but by raising the bar of the law, they were going to say, "There's no way we can do that. We need grace to love our enemies."

Like Jesus, I'm trying to move you from law to grace by telling you something contrary to what you were taught.

Because there's a marked tendency today, and it's been so deeply ingrained, to debate or make God's grace a two-way proposition. We feel that somehow, we're involved in what the Father does entirely by grace. The universal definition of grace is: His unmerited favor. Right? That's the one we all grew up with. But in that definition is an unspoken law that says His favor and blessing pivot on our obedience, receiving, believing, faith, etc. It's tied to something we do. In this book, I'm moving you from law to grace. I'm moving you from feeding from the tree of the knowledge of evil to the tree of life. You've heard it said that if we believe, receive, and have faith, God grants us favor. But I say unto you that any condition tied to grace makes it no longer grace. It makes it a wage or a merit. When you feel grace is contingent on what you do, no matter how small or minute, it's no longer grace. Any action at all, any doing on your part to get God to release His favor, goodness, and blessing, means you've just moved from grace into a mixture of works and grace. Can you see that?

If we truly accept that grace as His unmerited favor, it must be undeserved, unearned, unacted on, and unreceived on our part. It is just a gift.

Now, this is incredibly ingrained in those of us that come from a charismatic stream. Most of us from charismatic circles believe it's up to us to gather enough people in one place to pray hard enough to God. And only then will He unfold His arms and finally release what we have been praying and crying out for. And we've called that grace. That's not grace. We thought that our faith releases and receives grace. That's not grace. It may produce an emotional release that some mistake for God's presence. We thought if we could just pray our hearts out and pray it through, God could finally hear us. Because we eventually forged our way through all the garbage, and now have this clear, unpolluted line to God open. We *prayed through*. But all we had was an emotional release. Because God is omnipresent.

How do you *pray through* to Him when He's everywhere? How do you *pray through* to Him when you're never out of his presence? It's an emotional release. And honestly, it produces frustration and anxiety. Because to create that same release or spiritual high, you've got to do more *praying through* than you did the last time to get you there. It's like a drug. Taking more effort, more prayer, more travailing, more pushing, more balling, and more squalling. You're always pressing in. And have you noticed in that culture nothing that we were crying out for really happens? The move of God was always coming. It was just around the next corner. Always just about to break out at any time. We were told to just *press in and birth it*. But I say to you, we're not waiting on a "coming soon" move of God. You are the move of God. We're not looking for the move of God. We're looking at God moving in each of us.

I appreciate that grace moves us out of the anticipating and expecting, past trying to get enough people travailing to birth what God wants. Past pressing in for more. Grace moves us into the realization and manifestation of Christ from the tree of life within.

The entire history of mankind started in grace and will end in grace. God's one direction of grace, from Himself to man, without man's participation, vote, or declaration, started when He stamped all of us with His image and likeness. We did nothing to merit, deserve, or earn His image and likeness. He created all of us. Every person you encounter, from your favorite to your least favorite, is made in the image and likeness of God. None of us did anything to merit that. It was God giving it to us without our agreement or consent. It's who we are.

The Garden of Eden was the prototype grace gift. It came to man from God. He planted it, and He brought it to pass. God made full provision in the garden. He finished the work entirely. It was a perfect garden. There was nothing that needed to be added to it. And then God set man in the middle of this perfect garden. In the middle of this grace gift. Every grace gift God prepares, perfects, and brings it to its absolute zenith for us. And then He places us in the middle of it. Adam didn't *pray and lay hold* of the garden. He didn't *extend his faith* for the garden. He didn't *believe and receive it*. Another one I hear is, *yes, it's a gift, but you must unwrap it*. No, Adam didn't have to unwrap the gift of the garden. His belief in the garden didn't make it real. He didn't have to do any of those things we've religiously attached to the gift of grace. What did Adam do? He simply opened his eyes to see what already was. Seeing everything God had provided. He opened his eyes to see the full manifestation of this grace gift that he had nothing to do with preparing, finishing, or making complete. God simply set him in the middle of it to enjoy.

You have a garden planted in the very core of your being. And it's called the kingdom of God. It is within you. And within this garden is planted within you the tree of life. It is called the Christ within. And it is a one-way gift that God has given humanity. He has placed you in the kingdom. He did that at the resurrection of Jesus. All old things passed away, and all things became new at the resurrection. The Bible says He has delivered us from the power of darkness and translated us into the kingdom of God's dear Son. He did that all alone without your effort, approval, or decision. It was all His doing. He thoroughly prepared it and set you in the middle of it. All that is left for you to do is to open your eyes and see it. To come to a place of consciousness where you now see that everything that He has completely prepared for you is free of charge. It was simply given to you. You don't have to merit, earn, or deserve it. God simply placed you in the middle of it.

And as you eat from the tree of life, this Christ within, the awareness of everything He has done grows, expands, and enlarges. You don't have to *fast for it* or call for *an all-night prayer vigil*. You don't have to fill a stadium with people to *cry out for it*. It's not coming, so you don't have to *get ready, get ready, get ready*. Grace moves you past this always seeking, looking, and anticipating that it's just around the next corner. Grace moves you past a never achieving, never getting there kind of mentality. Past thinking that if we could do a little more, try harder, push out farther, and increase our faith, we would get there.

That's not grace. That's the fuel that drives religion.

You have a garden within you called the kingdom. It's not out there someplace. It's within you. It's called the tree of life, and it's the Christ who lives in you. In fact, Jesus said in Luke 9:27, *"I tell you truly, there are some standing here who shall not taste death until they see the kingdom of God."* Many religious church circles I used to travel in were always looking for the manifestation of the kingdom. But Jesus said, there are some of you standing here that will not taste death until you see the kingdom of God. So, either some really old folks are running around, or the kingdom is already here. I'm putting my bet on the kingdom already being here and that none of those folks standing there that day are still alive.

How does this kingdom work within us?

In Luke 17, the Pharisees asked Jesus when the kingdom of God would come. They were looking, like many people today, for an outward kingdom. They were looking for a kingdom that they could lay their eyes on. And so, they wanted to know when the kingdom would finally come. Jesus answered and said in verses 20-21, *"The kingdom of God does not come with observation. [21] Nor will they say, 'See here!' or 'See there!' For indeed, the kingdom of God is within you."*

> **The garden was given entirely by grace to Adam, and the kingdom garden was completely given to us by grace. It is a free gift.**

And there's something unique about the gifts God gives. When God gives a gift, He gives it. And He never takes it back. Paul said something mind-blowing in Romans 11:29, *for the gifts and the calling of God are irrevocable.* What does it mean that His gifts and calling are irrevocable? It means that you cannot earn them or do anything to get them. And it means He's already given them to you, **and you can't return them**. That's what irrevocable means. They're non-returnable. They are gifts of God, not works, lest any man boast. Notice that the gifts are plural, but there's only one call. He's called all of us. And then every gift He gives us, and there are lots of gifts He gives us, they are 100% irrevocable. We cannot return them.

So, here's something to think about. Did you know that since the resurrection, you can't get out of the Last Adam any easier than you could get out of the first Adam before the cross? Why? Because it's a gift from God. It's an irrevocable gift. So, *believing and receiving* involves eating from the tree of life. It is having a Christ in us awareness. And as you become more aware of Christ in you, that's when you believe. Believing is simply an agreement to what has already been established. Believing creates nothing. It merely agrees with an already established reality.

Faith is the substance of things hoped for. It is the evidence of things not seen. It does not just believe for something to be created out of thin air. There is evidence and a substance to faith. To believe for something, you must know it is an already established fact. But we thought that if we *believe to receive it*, it's suddenly created. It becomes real. No, no, no, no. The only thing you can believe for is for something already real. You can only receive what is already there.

So, all we do with our faith is discover what He already established in the garden by grace. Discovering what is irrevocable.

Eating from the tree of life on this side of the cross is seeing Christ within. And as we eat from this tree, we grow in grace, increasing in trust and love.

4

BRANCH OF TRUST - PART 1

For years, I thought I responded. I recognized the Holy Spirit stirring in me and speaking something. But my response was to think about it. And I would make a choice that seemed logical. Can you relate to that? I knew God was telling me something, but then I would run it through the filter of my understanding. And do you know why I did that? Because I made my will lord. Come on. That's just the truth. I made my will, my decision, sovereign. I would make the choice that seemed good to me and ask God to bless what I wanted. Do you see how convoluted we get by thinking that the tree of the knowledge of good and evil will guide us?

Do you know what I discovered? The knowledge of good has one too many o's. The knowledge of God has only one.

And we will never know liberty and freedom until we eat from the tree of life and cut the route to the knowledge of good. But to do that, you must be 100% convinced that God can deal with all the little intricacies and practicalities of your life better than you can. Religion has highly trained us to make good choices and get a good handle on things. That's the knowledge of good. But as you eat from the tree of life, no longer allowing your decisions to come from the knowledge of good and evil, the branch of trust flourishes. And you will notice three things happening in your life.

1. You respond to the Holy Spirit's initial stirring.

Instead of asking Him questions like, *Lord, what do I need to do? Do I need to take this job? Or do I need to move there? How? What do I do with my kids?* Or whatever the question is regarding what you're facing in life. If you quiet those questions and move out of your head and listen to your spirit, you will sense this internal stirring giving you direction. The tree of life in you, your life source, floods your heart with revelation. And as He floods your heart with revelation, you feel this stirring inside. And if you are living from the tree of life, you will respond to that initial stirring of the Spirit of God that lives in you.

We find that happening to Paul in the book of Acts when he's on the road to Damascus. Acts 9:1-2 (NKJV) says, *then Saul, still breathing threats and murders against the disciples of the Lord, ² went to the high priest and asked letters from him to the synagogues in Damascus so that if he found any who are of the way, whether men or women, he might bring them bound to Jerusalem.* Saul was eating from the tree the knowledge of good and evil. He was doing what he thought was right. He thought he was doing God's will. This was a learned man. Everything between good and evil, he knew well. So, he's doing what he thinks is good. But he is about to have a head-on collision with a tree called the Tree of Life.

Verses 3-6: *As he journeyed, he came near Damascus. And suddenly, a light shone round around him from heaven. ⁴ Then he fell to the ground and heard a voice saying to him, Saul, Saul, why are you persecuting Me? ⁵ And he said, Who are you, Lord? Then the Lord said, I am Jesus whom you're persecuting. It's hard for you to kick against the goads. ⁶ So he, trembling and astonished, said, Lord, what do you want me to do? Then the Lord said, Arise, go into the city, and you'll be told what you must do.*

Notice that when God's goodness and love appeared to Saul, he responded.

When God indeed shows Himself to you, you will respond. It won't take a preacher singing one more emotionally charged verse to pull you down to the altar to respond. We don't have to sing one more chorus of *waiting on you*. No. When He shines Himself on you, you will simply respond. There was no debate from Paul. He didn't reason within himself. *Is this right? Is this wrong? Let me think about it. Let me pray about it. Or I need a word from somebody.* The response to the tree of life is to drink deep from His revelation in us. And often, the response to revelation comes without mental awareness. When the Spirit of God stirs, we usually respond without being mentally aware that we're doing it. The tree of life puts you in a position of responding, not deciding. It doesn't put you in a place where you choose, evaluate, and weigh out the options.

Why? Because believing is a natural response to the tree of life's revelation in us. It is not something you can make yourself do. You can't make yourself believe anything. Believing happens when you see it and grasp it.

In Galatians, we find Paul responding again to the tree of life. Galatians 1:15-16 (NKJV) says, *but when it pleased God to separate me from my mother's womb and called me through His grace* [16] *to reveal His Son in me that I might preach Him among the Gentiles, I did not immediately confer with flesh and blood.*

When you get a revelation from God, it might be best to respond like Paul did and not confer with flesh and blood. Which is probably contrary to your religious upbringing. Paul responded. He didn't weigh it out or mentally figure out the options. And he didn't go to the apostles to get their input. He didn't need confirmation. When you get a revelation, you won't need confirmation either. Just crockpot it until you see the whole thing.

In Matthew Chapter 8, Jesus tells the people to follow Him. What's He doing? Looking for a response. He's moving them from law to grace, to eat from the tree of life. Instead, they go to the tree of the knowledge of good and evil. Matthew 8:18-21 (NKJV) says, *and when Jesus saw a great multitude about Him, He gave a command to depart to the other side.* [19] *Then, a certain scribe came and said to Him, "Teacher, I'll follow you wherever you go."* [20] *And Jesus said to him, "Foxes have holes, birds of the air have nests, but the Son of Man has nowhere to lay His head."* [21] *Then another of His disciples said to Him, Lord, "Let me first bury my father."* That seems like a good thing to do. It looks like a reasonable request. But what was Jesus' response?

Verse 22: *But Jesus said to him, "Follow me and let the dead bury their own dead."*

What was Jesus looking for? He was looking for an internal spirit response, not mental assent. Instead, they went and fed from the tree of the knowledge of good and evil. To this disciple, it seemed right. It seemed reasonable and proper to bury his daddy first. But Jesus was looking for a response out of his heart. The disciple didn't respond from the heart. Instead, he passed it through his head and the filters of the knowledge of good and evil.

Do you respond to His revelation or do a mental assent, weighing the options?

We've let knowledge be supreme long enough. It's time to realize that knowledge is not supreme. It is not power. And it is not life producing. And so, as we eat from the tree of life, what does it look like in our life? We respond to the initial leadings of the Holy Spirit. We trust in what the Holy Spirit speaks in us.

Let me use a term we are familiar with: you get a gut feeling.

Having a gut feeling is simply being led by the Spirit. You follow the Holy Spirit's prompting, His urging. It doesn't happen in your head through the accumulation of knowledge. It's an inner draw, an inner pull. This is where the Tree of Life communicates. He communicates in your spirit, not your head. But we're so used to feeding from the tree of the knowledge of good and evil that when we get something in our spirit, we run it through our heads. And if it doesn't make sense in our head, we refuse what the Tree of Life speaks in our spirit.

And that's a significant clue about which tree you're genuinely feeding from. If you get a prompt in your spirit but refuse to follow it because it makes little sense mentally, you are eating from the wrong tree.

Paul talks about this in Romans 8. He tells us what happens when we live according to the flesh. When we eat from the tree of the knowledge of good and evil. Flesh gets all its information and knowledge from your five senses. From what you see, hear, smell, taste, and touch. Those five senses feed knowledge to your mind. Then, you make what you think is a good decision based on your senses. And in verse 13 of Romans 8, Paul says that the consequence of living according to the flesh, or the knowledge of your senses, is that you'll die. And then, he talks about living by the spirit. It's translated capital S in most translations. But I'm not sure it should be a capital S. It is not capitalized in Greek. So, it's up to the translator to put it in there. Verse 13 says, *if you, by the spirit, put to death the deeds of the body, you will live.* In other words, if you stop listening to your flesh, and making decisions based on your senses, what you hear in your spirit will put to death what is being fed into your mind. You will live.

Life and death come from two different sources of knowledge and information. We choose how to live our life based on those two sources: the flesh (the tree of the knowledge of good and evil) and the spirit (or the tree of life.)

> **I'm not just talking about theology. I'm talking about your decisions about marriage, children, business, etc. Every decision you make comes from the source of one of those trees.**

Paul continues saying in verse 14, *For as many as are led by the Spirit of God.* This time it is capitalized in the Greek Interlinear. As many as are led by Holy Spirit. It doesn't say those who accumulate knowledge. The Holy Spirit communicates in us, leading our spirit. It says that *as many as are led by the Spirit of God are the sons of God.*

In First Corinthians 2:13, Paul said, *these things we also speak not in words which man's wisdom teaches.* He's drawing a contrast between the tree of the knowledge of good and evil and the tree of life. Just like the contrast, we read in Romans 8 between the flesh and the spirit. Paul says, "We're not speaking from the tree of the knowledge of good and evil. We're not speaking man's wisdom. We're speaking those words which the Holy Spirit or the Tree of Life teaches, comparing spiritual things with spiritual." But we find the dilemma in verse 14, which says that the natural, carnal man eating from the tree of the knowledge of good and evil does not receive things from the tree of life. Why? Because they are foolish to him. Why are they foolish to him? Because the five physical senses feed information to the mind in conflict with the Spirit's leading. In conflict with what the Tree of Life is teaching.

> *So now we've got a clash. Do we follow this inner prompting, this urging? Do we allow the Spirit to lead us? Or do we continue to filter these spirit promptings through our minds?*

Making decisions based on what seems logical to us? Or what seems reasonable to our senses?

It says the natural man does not receive the things of the Spirit of God. Do you see the contrast? They are foolish and senseless to him. We've sat in churches forever, desiring to be led by the Spirit but living by our minds. We want to follow as the Spirit leads us and be taught by the Spirit. But as soon as He shows us something in our spirit, we run it through our minds. And if it doesn't make sense mentally, we reject it. If it sounds foolish to our five physical senses, our experiences, and what we've heard from other sources, we completely shut it down. It builds tremendous trust when you follow these initial promptings of the Holy Spirit.

So let me tell you straight, don't pass what comes to your spirit through the filter of knowledge. If you do, I can assure you, you will move from the tree of life back to the tree of the knowledge of good and evil.

Let's go back to Romans chapter eight. And we're going to paraphrase, exchanging the word flesh for the tree of the knowledge of good and evil. Romans 8:5: *for those who live according to the tree of the knowledge of good and evil set their minds on the things of the tree of the knowledge of good and evil.* It's a setting of the mind. It's a learning and grasping from the mind. Paul continues in verse 5, saying *those who live according to their spirit have their minds set on living according to the Tree of Life.* They set their minds on the things of the tree of life. Verse six, *for good and evil minded, is death. But to have a mind fully set on the tree of life is life and peace.* What is Paul saying? If you want life and peace, you can't fix your mind on the tree of the knowledge of good and evil and accumulate more knowledge and understanding. Hoping that by gaining enough knowledge and understanding, you will make the right decisions and avoid wrong choices. Choosing the good and avoiding the evil. He said it doesn't work that way. You must focus on the one source where there is no duality.

This trying to figure out what is right, what is wrong, what is good, and what is evil has caused great confusion within the body of Christ. There is only one source we need to look at. There is one source of life, and it's not up to us to figure everything out. It is up to Him to lead us and feed us. Your head will constantly challenge what comes to your spirit. Your mind will continuously belittle your inner promptings because the tree of the knowledge of good and evil has gotten comfortable running the show. The tree of the knowledge of good and evil is used to being in control of your life. It does not want to yield to the Spirit of God. Head knowledge wants to be god. Haven't you figured it out yet? It wants to reign supreme. It doesn't want to yield to what comes in your spirit.

So first, we respond to the inner promptings telling our mind to be quiet and submit to our spirit. We don't run it through the filter of our minds. That's the wrong tree. There's one source of knowledge, wisdom, and life, J E S U S.

I wish I could tell you that your B I B L E was the complete source of life for you. But there are 25,000 different interpretations of it. And only one Truth will come to your spirit, and you'll learn to hear His voice. His sheep hear His voice. Jesus said when He, the Spirit of Truth, has come, He will lead you into all truth. I love my Bible. But Jesus never said a book would lead you into all truth. I thank God for revelation and understanding, but there is one Spirit of Truth. And if you're looking to your B I B L E to figure out what's right and wrong, good, and evil, then you're eating from the wrong tree.

You simply need to listen to what goes on inside.

5
BRANCH OF TRUST - PART TWO

In the last chapter, we looked at what happens when you eat from the tree of life. As the branch of trust flourishes in your life, the first thing you'll notice is that you follow the inner promptings of the Holy Spirit. Let's continue looking at what happens as you trust the leading of the Holy Spirit.

The second thing you'll notice is:

2. You embrace His will, even when you don't know what it is.

Embracing His will even when you don't know what it is develops trust. The tree of the knowledge of good and evil wants to know everything about His will before embracing it. This tree hates mystery. It is obsessed with knowing and won't move until it knows. As a pastor, I often heard people say things like, *well, I just don't know if I feel led to do such and such.* It's because we want to figure it out. Knowledge is the lord in our lives, and we must have it all figured out before responding. We tend to be control freaks, don't we? We want to be like God, knowing the end from the beginning. Before we ever start the venture.

Jesus said in John 4:34, *"My meat, My food is to do the will of Him who sent Me and to finish His work."* There was some time between being sent and finishing. And maybe in the natural understanding, He didn't know it all, didn't understand it. But this He knew: **what the Father sent Him to do, He would finish it.** And all God is saying to us is, "Look, whatever I have sent you to do, we will get it done, one step at a time. You don't have to know it all." When you eat from the tree of life, you follow His will even when you don't know all of it. Even when you don't know where it's taking you. Do you see complete trust in that? When you eat from the tree of life, the branch that grows out it's called T R U S T. You trust Him. You're not trusting yourself. When he leads you, you follow His prompting. You may not know all of it, you may not know how it's all gonna work out, or what the end will be, but you follow even when you don't know where you're going. That shows trust.

For example, in Genesis chapter 12, God shows up to this idol worshiper in Mesopotamia named Abram. And he was not a godly man, by the way. And the Lord said to Abram, *"Get out of your country, from your family."* That will startle you. Right? You've lived in one city, one region all your life. Your family's rooted there. And God shows up and says, I want you to get out of your country and get away from your family. What do you do? *You probably think, well, that can't be God. It doesn't sound reasonable at all. I should... [fill in the blank.]* Or you say, "I bind you, devil, in the name of Jesus."

. . .

And then God says to Abram, *"Not only from your family and from your father's house but to a land that I will show you."* Well, where are we going? God says, "Look, you're gonna have to trust me. I'm not telling you; I'm showing you. I'm feeding you from this tree of life. And you're gonna have to follow My will even though you don't know what it is and where it's going to take you." And then He gives Abram a promise. Verse 2: *"I'll make you make you a great nation. I'll bless you and make your name great. And you shall be a blessing. I will bless those who bless you and curse those who curse you. And in you all the families of the earth shall be blessed."* Then it says in verse 4 that Abram departed just as the Lord had spoken to him. But did he leave precisely as the Lord had spoken? No. The last part of verse 4 says, *and Lot went with him.* What did God tell him? Get away from your family. But to the tree of the knowledge of good and evil, it only seemed fitting to take somebody along. You got to have a traveling buddy. Right? I can just hear Abram reasoning it out, "Come on God. I'm gonna take my nephew Lot. There's nothing wrong with that. It seems reasonable to me."

The benchmark to the tree of life way of living is to follow even when you don't know where you're going. Choosing based on what you know is eating from the wrong tree. However, if you follow when you're unsure where you're going, then it's Him making the call. He sets the direction. And the good news is that if He makes the call and sets the direction, then He's the one that's responsible for getting you where He's taking you. This is where trust comes in, and everything that's breaking around you doesn't move you. You aren't driven by all the news and reports or by what your five senses tell you.

Paul said in 2 Corinthians 4:18: *We don't look at the things that are seen.* When you eat from the tree of life, you can't depend on the things seen. He said we look at the things that are not seen. The things that are seen feed your mind. Which is information from the wrong tree. So, what do we do? We look at the things that are not seen, what He's speaking to our spirit.

We don't look at the things seen because they are temporary. Meaning that they are subject to change.

How often have we had decisions based on what we see end up trapping us? Then two weeks later, the circumstances changed. Now we're confused and upset, and we must make more decisions based on the new "changed" circumstances. And so, what do we typically do? We go back to the tree of the knowledge of good and evil and say, "I better get on the internet and Google this because I need to see what to do. I need more knowledge. Because if I can get more knowledge, I'll make the right decision." So, we find what we're looking for and make another decision. Do you know what happens then? Circumstances change again! And now we're really in a quandary. We're looking for more knowledge to make more decisions, and circumstances keep changing, requiring more knowledge and choices. And we're stuck in this cycle of instability. If you feed from the tree of life, you will become stable and fixed on what He has told you in your spirit. And you can set your course on that will, even though you don't know where you're going. And you'll no longer be moved by those things that you see.

So, eating from the tree of the knowledge of good and evil is about making continual adjustments based on circumstances. And eating from the tree of life is embracing what He speaks in your spirit, and remaining consistent, trusting Him.

Let him tell you what to do.

Sometimes we eat from the tree of life and follow His will. We don't know where we're going, but we follow it. But when what we see gets strong enough, we end up running back to the wrong tree. Abraham did that. Let's go back to Genesis 12. We're told that Abraham leaves with Lot. He fed from the tree of the knowledge of good and evil and took Lot with him. And you know, anytime you feed from that tree, things don't work out. And he and Lot ended up going separate ways, and they split up all the provisions. Abraham gave Lot the choice of which direction to take. And so, Lot chose which way he wanted to go and left. And then we're told in Genesis chapter 12:7, *And the Lord appeared to Abraham and said, "to your descendants, I will give this land."*

Abraham arrived at the land that was promised. And he builds an altar to the Lord, who had appeared to him. So far, everything is looking good. Abraham followed God's will, even though he didn't know where he was going, and he finally arrived, built an altar, and worshiped God. So far, so good. But suddenly, this circumstance arises in the land that God promised him. And then, we find in verse 10 a famine in the land. If God has given you the land, He's given you the provision. You can trust that He will take care of you. Despite the contradicting circumstance, God has supplied everything you will need in the promise. He already promised Abraham that He had given him the land. Abraham had a prompting in his spirit, hearing the Spirit of God. And he followed that prompting, following God's will even when he didn't know where he was going. And then, he gets to the place where the promise should be, and there is a famine.

> **This often happens to us. We arrive at the destination, at the promise, but something contrary pops up.**

So, what did Abraham do then? Did he stay with the tree of life? No, he ran back to the tree of the knowledge of good and evil. Verse 10 tells us he went to Egypt to dwell there, *for the famine was severe in the land.* Did God say it was severe? No, I guess Abraham thought it was severe. Was it a big problem for God? No. It was a big problem for Abraham. It was a big problem in his mind. So, he switched out of his spirit and back into his mind. Are you with me?

> **What do you do when a conflict arises between the Tree of Life's promise and what you see? Do you dance with the one that brought you? Or do you head back to the other tree?**

Jesus was trying to teach his disciples that very thing in Matthew Chapter 14. Jesus had just finished an all-day teaching session, and it was getting to be late in the afternoon. And in verse 15, it says, *When it was evening, his disciples came to Him and said, "This is a deserted place, and the hour is already late. Send the multitudes away so they can go into the villages and buy themselves food."* That seemed a reasonable, logical, good thing to do. Right? But in Verse 16, Jesus said, *"They don't need to go away. You give them something to eat."* Now we've got a conflict between the two trees. The tree of the knowledge of good and evil is saying it's late at night, and they need to leave and go home. But we've got a prompting from the Tree of Life that says, No, they don't need to go. I've made provision for them. You give them something to eat. You take care of the need. So now what do we do?

Let's look at verse 17 and I'll paraphrase it, adding in the trees. *Reasoning in their minds and eating from the tree of the knowledge of good and evil, they said to Him, "We've only got five loaves and two fish. There's no way we can feed all of them."* Verse 18, *the Tree of Life Himself says, "Bring them to me." And He commanded them all to sit down on the grass. He took the five loaves and two fish, and looking up to heaven, He blessed and broke them and gave the loaves to the disciples, and the disciples gave to the multitude. So, they all ate and were filled. And they took up twelve baskets full of the fragments that remained.*

Personally, I believe there was a basket for each disciple to remind them which tree they needed to go to in the future.

Now those who had eaten were about 5,000 men. And I'm assuming they were married, which would increase the number to 10,000. And let's say each couple had two kids [which would be an average Western American family today]. So, there were about 20,000 people that were fed. The question is: which tree fed them? The tree of the knowledge of good and evil or the tree of life? It was the Tree of Life that fed them.

When the Tree of Life spoke to the twelve, it didn't seem possible for them. So, they went to the tree of the knowledge of good and evil. And ran what the Tree of Life had said through the filter of their mind. They said, "We've only got five loaves and two fish; what are they among so many?" They totally disregarded what the Tree of Life spoke to them, "You feed them." What should they have done? Started breaking the five loaves and two fish and watched the supernatural multiplication of provision occur. We are to follow His will, even though we don't know where it's taking us. They didn't have to know the end from the beginning. All He asked them to do was follow His will. The Tree of Life fed the 20,000 people there that day. The other tree did not. Why? Because the tree of the knowledge of good and evil will always fall short. But the Tree of Life will always carry through.

3. You recognize your union with the Father through the Son in the Holy Spirit.

This tree of life is a tree of union. You're not in this thing alone. God did not create you to live independently from Him. He didn't design you to strive and get knowledge apart from Him. You weren't meant to eat at the tree of the knowledge of good and evil, reading books, and studying day and night to make yourself omniscient so you can be like God. While the Father, Son, and Holy Spirit are over here with Their arms crossed, saying "We'll just wait till he gets desperate enough and cries out for Us." No. There is no separation. We are in union with Him. Knowing and embracing this simple truth that you are included in Them. This circle of relationship is Father, Son, Holy Spirit, and you. You're joined with Them. You are hand in hand with them.

And you know what that knowledge does? It lets us take a deep breath and relax because we know we are in union with Him and that everything will work fine.

However, the tree of the knowledge of good and evil hates union. Why? Because it's rooted in the lie of separation, it always pushes a mindset of **doing to become.** While union says, "There is nothing you have to do to become because you already are." So, until we understand this union we have, we will keep going back to the tree of the knowledge of good and evil to find out what we need to **do to become.**

You share the intimacy that the Triune God shares. They have included you in Their union. Your mission and the mission of the Father, Son, and Holy Spirit are all different, yet we're in communion. We're in union, one with another. Trusting in that settles you down. When you know you're one with Him, it quiets your emotions. After all, what greater security could you have than knowing you're in union with Them? That's the prayer that Jesus prayed, "That they may be one as You, Father, are in Me and I in you that they may be one in Us." And Jesus prayed that pre-cross to His disciples that they might know then that they were one with Them? How does that work? It works like this: the Father speaks to the Son, the Son speaks to the Holy Spirit, and the Spirit leads you into all truth. That's how the tree of life works.

Again, we're not just talking about this working in theology. This works in the practicalities of life. It works in your marriage. Do you want wisdom for your marriage? Let the Father speak to the Son, the Son to the Spirit, and let the Spirit lead you into all truth. Do you need to make a business decision? Let the Father speak to the Son, the Son to the Spirit, and let the Spirit speak to you and lead you into truth. Should you buy that house or not? Again, let the Father speak to the Son, the Son to the Spirit, and let the Spirit speak to you and lead you into all truth.

. . .

Do you need to know what to do with your rebellious, out-of-control kids? Rather than reading child-rearing books and getting wisdom from the so-called "experts," go to the Tree of Life. And let the Father speak to the Son, and the Son speak to the Spirit, and let the Spirit speak to you and lead you into all truth. The Spirit always defers to the Son, and the Son always points to the Father. There's a different mission and function, but They are in union together and have included you in Their union.

Your flow from the Father to the Son to the Spirit to you comes into your spirit. Into this divine nature. Did you know the Bible says you are a partaker of the Divine nature? How is that possible? Because Genesis 1:26 says, *you are created in the image and the likeness of God.* So, when the tree of life speaks, it speaks to that image. It speaks to the likeness of God with whom you are in union. The problem we've had in the church is that believers and pre-believers that eat at the tree of the knowledge of good and evil live no differently than one another. Believers have been eating at the same tree from which the world's been eating. But we should take advantage of the tree of life in us. We've been trying to become smarter than the world. There are many sharp people out there, but none are as sharp as my Dad. And Dad speaks to the Son who speaks to the Spirit who speaks to me and leads me into all truth. Then I live from the mind of Christ. And when that happens, nobody's as bright as I am. That's the truth. He will take you where you need to go.

Romans 8:17: *and if children, then heirs—heirs of God and joint heirs with Christ.* That verse smacks of union to me. It smacks of a family being one together. It goes on and says *if indeed we suffer with Him that we also may be glorified together.* And verse 19 is where we now show ourselves differently from the world. The reason we haven't differed from the world because we've been eating from the same tree they have. We've been trying to get more knowledge. The only difference between us and the world is that we've been trying to sit and ponder and figure out this Bible for years and generations. And we've allowed this to cause division and strife and 25,000 denominations, all of which have the corner on truth because they have more knowledge. And we're trying to tell everybody else what their knowledge is.

And meanwhile, nobody's getting a life. The Bible is not the life-giver. Jesus is the life giver! I get a lot out of the Bible. I love it. Every day I read it. But listen, it is not the tree of life. King Jesus is the tree of life. Let me put it this way: In King Jesus, I rest, and in King James, I read. So, when we eat from the tree of life, we trust God.

So, Romans 8 verse 17 tells us who we are. And then verse 19 says [my paraphrase], *For the earnest expectation of the creation eagerly waits for the revealing of the sons who eat from the tree of life.* That's what the world is looking for, something that works. Something that's not just fluffed over, saying it's better than what they have and yet has no demonstration of it. It's the tree of life that all creation is looking for. And verse 21 [my paraphrase] says *creation will also be delivered from the bondage of corruption. Set free from the corrupt tree of the knowledge of good and evil. They are delivered into the glorious liberty of the children of God.* The pre-believing world will find their freedom as a child of God when they see you eating from a different tree than what they're eating from. They will awaken to what they have seen through the tree we feed from, realizing that it's more than just knowledge. Their awakening, their eye-opening, will come through you simply being connected to the right tree and expressing the life of that tree.

God, help us in this generation to express the life of the right tree to a pre-believing world.

Remember, Paul said, I've discovered that God separated me from my mother's womb. It really pleased God to reveal the Christ within me. Then he said it was his ministry's mission to reveal that Christ is in all the Gentiles. The Christ within feeds your heart from the tree of life. And we'll call heart, spirit, and gut feeling all the same, just for the sake of simplicity, in this book. The Christ, the Tree of Life within, feeds your heart, your spirit man. But the senses feed the mind. When Eve saw the fruit, it looked good to her eyes. Her eyes fed knowledge to her head and said, *I must have that.* And when her head said, *yes, I want that,* agreeing with what her eyes were seeing, she made a wrong decision. She disconnected from the tree of life and connected to the tree of the knowledge of good and evil. She joined with the wrong tree.

The mind, fed by the senses, loves the tree of the knowledge of good and evil. Why? Because that tree promises to make us like God. That tree says you can be large and in charge, and your will reigns supreme. God, Himself will not violate your free will if you just learn right.

How's that working for you?

So, the mind resists what the tree of life through the heart or the spirit reveals. And it comes with doubts. It comes with questions. The Spirit of God prompts us in our spirit. And the mind says, No, no, no. And it gives us doubts and questions. The mind has got to be renewed to bow to what Christ within has revealed to the heart. And when it does, trust is built. And you begin then to obey the initial leadings of the Holy Spirit. You follow His will and even though you don't know where it's taking you, you go on the journey. You rest in your union with the Father, through the Son, in the Spirit. And that will move you past your doubts. And that will empower you in every area of your life, bar none.

He has given you everything that pertains to life and godliness through the tree of life. Not through the tree, the knowledge of good and evil. Wherever you need help, wherever you need understanding and wisdom, I'm urging you that the Spirit of God today is taking us from one tree to the other. He's moving us in mass to the right tree. And you're gonna trust that leading on the inside. Those who are led, not taught, but led by the Holy Spirit, are the sons of God. Let the leading, the prompting, the inner pull of the Spirit of God shut this carnal mind down. Because if you don't, you're going to follow what you see and what you hear. You're going to follow what everybody else is doing. And when you get to where circumstances change, as Scripture says they will, you will need to revamp your decisions. And you will live a life that is up and down all the time. When your choices are working, you're up. And when they're not, you're down. You're in today and out tomorrow. You're loving Jesus today, but you're confused tomorrow. Why? Because we keep plugging into the wrong tree.

And that branch of trust, as you eat at the tree of life, causes you to rest in Him. You lean back into Him. In all your ways, acknowledging Him, trusting Him in everything you do. And He keeps your heart and mind settled. Starving the two branches that grow from the tree of the knowledge of good and evil: the branches of performance and fear. When you rest and trust in Him, you stop performing to please Him. And when you stop performing to please Him, all fear vanishes. Why? Because your fears were based on your inability to perform at a level you thought would please Him.

6

BRANCH OF LOVE

The branch of love is the other branch that grows out of this tree of life. And let me say from the start, if it's not pure and unconditional love, then it's not growing out of the tree of life. The only love that grows out of the tree of life is in Christ. The tree of life is the Christ within. And as we become increasingly aware of Him and that awareness expands, our love for the Father grows until this limb is enormous. 1 John chapter 4:18 says, *there is no fear in love*. If there's anything you fear from God, then it's not pure love. He is love. Do you understand that there is no fear in God?

When people who claim to love God fear Him, it's not pure love. That's not what He's looking for. There is no fear in love. Perfect Love Himself, the Tree of Life, will drive out fear. Perfect Love casts out any fear you have, such as death, disease, or lack. It drives out all fears because fear involves torment. I know many believers today who are terrified of God because they think God will torment them if they don't please Him. No. God torments nobody. I don't know how we came up with that. God does not torment anybody. How can Love torment? There is no torment in love. John goes on in v. 18 and 19, saying *fear involves torment, but he who fears has not been made perfect or mature in love* [19] *We love Him because He first loved us.*

How does the limb of love growing out of the tree of life, out of the Christ within, work? As you become more aware of Him and your focus is on Him, this love grows and becomes enormous. It's an awareness that we love Him because He first loved us.

As you read this book, I want you to know that as you become more aware of the Christ within, you will no longer tell God how much you love Him in order to convince Him so that He can finally love you back. Has anybody ever been in that cycle? *If I can just tell him how much I love him. If I could just convince him. Then He'll respond and love me too.* No. As we feed on this tree of life, this branch of love grows strong. Why? Because I recognize that my love for Him is just a response to this overwhelming love, He has always had for me. If you're going to focus on your love relationship with God, don't focus on how much you love him. Focus on how much He has always loved you. Meditate on it. Ponder it. Let that love branch grow. Don't even one time tell him how much you love Him? Just let Him love you.

And as you ponder and think about that all-consuming love He has for you, you're gonna find love for Him just wells up within you. You don't have to crank it up. You don't have to work at convincing Him. He is the source of love. You're not the source of love trying to convince Him how much you love Him so that He will love you back. He's overwhelming you and overpowering you with His love. And your love for Him is simply a response. It's that love that Paul said compelled him. And it is what compels me. I tried to be motivated for years by my love for Him. I just wanted to do so much because of my great love for Him. Because of my faithfulness to love Him. No, no, no, no. It's His endless love for us that compels and motivates us.

In the last two chapters, we talked about the branch of trust empowering us to do three things.

1. To respond to the promptings of the Holy Spirit.

2. To enable you to embrace God's will for you, even when you don't know all it is.

3. And it helps you see you are in union with the Father through the Son in the Spirit.

And this big love branch also empowers you and compels you into action as you feed from the Tree of Life. What kind of actions? Three love responses flow from you as His love overwhelms you.

1. You'll be available to serve Him no matter the job.

Knowledge reigns supreme in the tree of the knowledge of the good and evil world. It makes us feel God is pleased as we serve Him. So, we serve to please God. But the Tree of Life energizes and motivates us because His love reigns supreme and compels us. The other tree makes us feel like we must do something. For example, we haven't been to church in months, but we're scheduled to serve as greeters this week. So, we need to go. God will be pleased with our serving.

He will be pleased with the sacrifice we make. However, the Tree of Life energizes you and motivates you so that you want to. There's a world of difference between having to and wanting to. You want to because of the revelation of His vast love for you. And without you even recognizing it, love compels you. It motivates you to serve.

What was it that caused Jesus to do what he did? In Mark 10:43- 45, Jesus tells us the difference between having to and wanting to. And in verse 43, He says, *"It shall not be so among you, but whosoever desires to be great among you, he shall be your servant."* We've read that and thought, *Oh, yeah, I've got to serve. I have to.* And in verse 44, He said, *"Whosoever of you desires to be first shall be slave of all."* And we've thought *Oh, that sounds too cumbersome. I'm not into that.* But Jesus said in verse 45, *For even the Son of Man.* So, you see, He came to do, not because He had to, but because He wanted to. It was His heart. It was who He was.

When we eat from this tree of life, this branch of love will grow large as we serve, not because we must, but because we want to. Why? Because Jesus set the standard. He said, *"I didn't come to be served but to serve. And to give My life a ransom for many."* Not because He had to. He left heaven because He desired to. He made himself of no reputation, not because He had to, He wanted to. And what made Him want to? He was one with Love. He was Love in manifestation. And it was that love that compelled Him to come to do what He wanted to do. Not because he was driven or forced to by any higher authority. And He didn't come on a guilt trip. He came purely out of a motivation of love.

Paul, in Galatians 5:22-23, is talking about the fruit of the Spirit. And really, he's talking about the fruit of the tree of life. He lists nine fruits. And the first one is love. He said, *But the fruit of the Spirit is love, joy, peace, long-suffering, kindness, goodness, faithfulness [23] gentleness, self-control.* Notice the first one is love. All the rest come out of love. If you pull the love fruit out, you'll never have joy, peace, long-suffering, kindness, goodness, faithfulness, gentleness, or self-control. All the other eight come out of this big one, which is love.

You eat from the tree of life, this Christ within, as His life. Because Jesus didn't come just for you, He came as you. The life that you're living, you're not living for Him. You're living as Him. You and He have become one Spirit. Paul said in 1 Corinthians 6:17 that *he who is joined to the Lord is one spirit.* So, there is no difference in what motivates your life or His life. You're living out of the same spirit of motivation that motivated Jesus. And the nine fruits of the spirit, the first of which is love, motivated Him. It characterized His life.

The way we increase in love is a Christ awareness that grows on the inside.

Feeding from the tree of life, the branch of love expresses the 'want to service.' And the 'have to' of the tree of the knowledge of good and evil is silenced. The attitude of the tree of the knowledge of good and evil is: what have you done for Me lately? It tells us the minimum that we need to do to be blessed by God. The tree of life reflects what the tree is, which is love. And the Tree of Life always sacrifices when it wants to, as it sees the need to fulfill what somebody else needs. Not because we must. But because we have fed on the tree of life. We have fed on the Christ within and are complete. The love we have fed on compels us to do it.

. . .

So, love compels me to do the job, whatever the job is. There are no big jobs, no little jobs in the kingdom. They're all equal.

2. Pleasing others is no longer an idol.

When you eat at the tree of life, you stop feeling like you must please others. Loving and serving others is different from pleasing others. And this is something I must watch because I can become a people pleaser. I like everybody to be happy. And I tend to do whatever I need to make everybody happy. My wife calls me Mr. Bobblehead because all I know how to do is say yes. Why do we become people pleasers? Because we need to be liked, we need to be loved.

But the problem is when you please people, you're looking for love in all the wrong places.

Paul faced this in ministry. In Galatians chapter one, he was confronted, and some problems arose because he was preaching the gospel. And in Galatians 1:9, he says, *so now I say again, if anyone preaches any other gospel to you than what we have preached to you, let him be accursed.* Why did he say that? Verse 10, *for do I now persuade men or God? Do I seek to please men? For if I still pleased men, I would not be a bondservant of Christ.*

And Jesus faced it with His family. In Mark 3:31, Jesus is teaching, and His brothers and mother came and stood outside, sending word to Jesus to come out to them. They said, "Go and tell Jesus, mom, and the boys are here." And so here is Jesus, teaching and in the middle of everything. He's moving and grooving, zigging, and zagging, unveiling revelation. And verse 32 says, *a multitude was sitting around Him, and they said to Him, "Look, Your mother and brothers are outside seeking You."* Then in verse 33, *Jesus answered them and said, "Who is My mother, or My brothers?"*

Can't you just see it? I bet mama's hair on the back of her neck stood up when He said that. She's thinking *the boy still ain't too big to whoop! What do you mean, who's your mother? Who is your mother?! Do you know who you're talking to? Hmm.* Verses 34-35, He looked around in a circle at those who sat about Him and said, "Here is My mother and My brothers [35] For whoever does the will of God is My brother and My sister and mother."

So even in Jesus' life, there were opportunities to be a people pleaser. But if He were to please His mama and brothers, He would have to drop everything He was doing and say, "Guys, hold on a second. I'll be right back." Like when your cell phone rings, you're with somebody, and you say, "Excuse me, just a minute, I gotta get the phone." Right? He would have said, "Excuse me, just a minute. I gotta go see what mom wants." He was under the same pressure, but Jesus knew that pleasing others and serving others were different.

And I love this one in John chapter seven. This is another time that Jesus had a run-in with His family. John 7:1 says, *After these things, Jesus walked into Galilee for He did not want to walk in Judea because the Jews sought to kill Him.* Smart move, right? You don't want to go through that. You don't want to go walking through the hood. They're looking for you to kill you. It says, *Now the Jews' Feast of Tabernacles was at hand.* So, his brothers, the smart alecks that they are and said to Him in verse 3, *"Depart from here and go into Judea that Your disciples also may see the works that You're doing."* What are they doing? They were tempting him. But He had just said, "I'm not going to Judea because they're looking to kill Me." But His brothers are telling Him, "Go on into Judea and show them who You are. They want to see the works. Right?"

And in verse four, they said, *"For nobody does anything in secret while he seeks to be known openly."* In other words, they're saying, Come on, big brother Jesus, if you want everybody to know who You are, why are You skirting around town? Why are you staying in secret? This is how everybody's gonna know. If You do these things and show Yourself to the world." And it says in verse five, *"For even His brothers did not believe Him."* If Jesus had been seeking to please His brothers, He would have said, "Okay, let's go to Judea and show them My power. We'll just zap them all if we need to. Let's go." But He didn't do that because He knew pleasing people is not the same as loving and serving people.

But here's the problem: nobody likes rejection.

We all like to be accepted. We all want to be the good guy. But if you minister this a non-mixed message of law and grace (of do to be, just believe and receive) there will be times in serving people the truth that you will not please them. Paul's message was of the finished work. A message of pure, radical grace and unconditional love. It saw no man after the flesh and understood that God loves us all the same and has reconciled us to Himself. In preaching that message, in serving people that truth, there will be moments that you don't please them.

. . .

This branch of love feeds you life and love for all men. And so, when you look at people, you're serving rather than pleasing, you'll know them not by their words or actions but through the filter of grace. And without that branch of love that grows in your life, the Christ within, you will not give that kind of grace to other people. Because the Tree of Life enables you to respond with the love you have received.

3. You'll watch visible difficulties and failures become the most incredible springboard to your growth.

I want to show you an example from the life of Jesus and his disciples. You know this story well. In Luke Chapter 8, Jesus had just finished teaching and said, "Let's hop in the boat and get to the other side." Verse 22, *Now it happened on a certain day that He got into a boat with His disciples. And He said to them, "Let us cross over to the other side of the lake."* Now, what did the Tree of Life feed them? What did He say? **Let us go over to the other side**. And they launched out. Verse 23 says, *But as they sailed, Jesus fell asleep.* See, when you're eating from the Tree of Life, the branch of love allows you to rest. So, the Tree of Life spoke, and He went to the back of the boat and took a nap. He's not worried. Why? Because He knows they are all going to the other side.

When the Tree of Life says you're going to the other side, you can sleep in the back of the boat and be confident that you are going to the other side.

But here's the problem. A windstorm came down on the lake. And here comes the tree of the knowledge of good and evil. It always tries to challenge what the Tree of Life says. The tree of the knowledge of good and evil feeds you or speaks to you through your senses. This tree comes through what you see, hear, touch, taste, and smell. It comes through the five physical senses. So, the five physical senses pick up on this windstorm on the lake. The Tree of Life said, "We're going to the other side." But the tree of the knowledge of good and evil said, "We've got a problem." Now, what are we going to believe? Are we going to believe the Tree of Life's words to us, or will we eat from the tree of the knowledge of good and evil?

They should have just gone to the back of the boat, laid down with Jesus, and laughed at the storm.

Remember, two big branches grow out of the tree of the knowledge of good and evil. One branch is performance, and the other is fear. Watch what happens when they eat from the wrong tree.

Verse 23 says, *a windstorm came down on the lake, and they were filling with water and were in jeopardy.* So, it's not written in this story, but I can tell you that the performance that went on here is that those guys had two-pound coffee cans and were bailing water. They were performing as hard and fast as they could go. Trying to keep that boat afloat. And they forgot what Jesus said, "We're going to the other side." They were just trying to stay up on the right side of the water.

. . .

And it says they were in jeopardy. Who said they were in jeopardy? Did the Tree of Life say they were in jeopardy? No. The tree of the knowledge of good and evil fed them the knowledge that they were in jeopardy. It told them they were in trouble and going to drown because of what they saw and heard. Verse 24, *and they came to Jesus, and they woke Him saying Master, Master, we are perishing.* How often do we go to God and tell him the exact opposite of what the Tree of Life has told us? And instead, carry Him information that we have from the tree of the knowledge of good and evil? Expecting Him to do something with the knowledge from the tree of good and evil when He's already told us how it would be from the tree of life. We're going to the other side!"

For example, the tree of Life says God was in Christ reconciling the world unto Himself. But the tree of the knowledge of good and evil says, *yeah, but that guy's really bad over there. And there ain't NO WAY God reconciled him. That's the worst desperado who ever walked on the face of the earth, so don't even try to tell me God reconciled him. There is no possible way.* But the Tree of Life said God was in Christ reconciling the world to Himself. The world means all men.

So, the disciple went over to Him, and they said, "Don't you care what's going on here? We're perishing." And the Tree of Life arose and rebuked the wind and the raging water, and they ceased. And there was calm. Verse 25 says, *but He said to them, "Where is your faith?"* Faith is a recognition of an established fact. The established fact was they were going to the other side. All faith needed to do was recognize what the fact was. So, Jesus isn't getting on their case about trying to conjure up enough faith to rebuke the storm or to stand firm and get their shield of faith and quench every fiery dart of the wicked one. He's just saying, recognize what I have told you. That is your faith. So, Jesus said, Where is your faith? Why are you afraid? And so, they marveled, saying one to another, who can this be? They didn't recognize Christ. Often, we don't recognize Christ within either. We don't recognize all He has put in us. Luke continues in verse 25, *for He commands, even the winds and the water, and they obey Him.*

So, here's my question: who had the actual power, Jesus, or the storm?

The disciples were giving power to the storm that it never had. And we give power to things that have no power. There is only one power. There is no lesser power that a greater power is trying to overcome. The storm had no power. The only power the storm had was what the disciples gave to it. There's one source, one power, one mind, one spirit, and one faith. The storm had no power. Some things arise in our lives, and we fear. And we bail as fast as we can, and we run to Jesus and say, "Don't you care that we're perishing?" And Jesus says, "What is the established fact? Why don't you rest on that?"

Jesus is the only power.

The Tree of Life said, we're going to the other side, and the tree, the knowledge of good and evil, said, we're going to perish. The performance was bailing and fretting. And then fear came. Fear is the other branch that grows out of the tree of the knowledge of good and evil.

They would have been fine if they could have successfully bailed enough water with their two-pound coffee cans to get to the other side. But they couldn't do it; it was overwhelming. And when problems overwhelm you and your performance inevitably fails, fear comes that you're perishing. You know what, these guys were sailors. They were fishermen and could have just rested and trusted in His love. They could have enjoyed the storm and said, "Let's stay here, and let's just see how bad this sucker can blow. Because we've already got the Word, we're going to the other side. So, fire your best shot storm because it doesn't matter. Fill the boat up with water till it's over the top. It doesn't matter. We're going to the other side."

Listen, we're all faced with a tree of the knowledge of good and evil and the Tree of Life's conflicting reports. The question is, whose report do you give the power to? Where is your focus? What are you conscious of? If you become mindful of the storm, the storm will be the power. If you become aware of the Christ within, Christ has the power?

Which force are you empowering, the storm or the Savior?

Through grace, we can watch the storm rage and the boat fill, but we can rest, trust, and believe because the Tree of Life has fed us fully. The tree of life has given us the word that His love never fails. His love will get us to the other side.

When you bring the branch of secure trust and this branch of love together, there is one overriding trait that the tree of life will have: an absolute obsession to know Him. This trust and love create this obsession to know Him better. Not knowing about him. But to know Him. Paul experienced that in Philippians chapter three. To intimately know Him and have this connection to where there's only one tree you eat from. There's only one source you look to and only one power that rules your life. Everything else is nothing. Everything else is zero. Paul said in Philippians 3:7, *but what things were gain to me, these I have counted loss for Christ.* And he goes on in verse 8 and says, *yet indeed I also count all things loss for the excellence of the knowledge of Christ Jesus my Lord, for whom I have suffered the loss of all things.* That doesn't mean he had nothing. That means everything else in comparison measured zero on the scale. He said I've got it all if I have His knowledge.

Everything He has given us comes by grace; when you have Him, you have everything. You don't have to worry about your health, money, future, spouse, or even if there will even be a spouse. We worry so much. Then Paul said, I've suffered the loss of all things and count them as rubbish. Which is a very nice conservative translation. The translators should have just put el toro poo-poo. It would've been more accurate. *I count them as el toro poo-poo so that I may gain Christ.* And he goes on in verse 9 and says, *and be found in Him, not having my own righteousness which is from the law.* Or you could say, which is from this tree of the knowledge of good and evil. And the last part of the verse says, *But that which comes through the faith in Christ.* Most translations say in Christ. But King James gets the correct preposition in there, and it changes the whole verse. **That which comes through the faith of Christ.** Not by your faith in Christ.

When you return to it being about your faith in Christ, it's about what you **do to become**. But what gets you through is His faith. My faith is in His faith. I have tremendous faith in His faith, but I've got no faith in my faith. And I lived for years trying to have faith in my faith, but it didn't work. But life flowed when I got faith in His faith and switched the trees I was eating from. And things start to work differently. So, in knowing Him, I get to know myself. That's what's so wonderful about it.

It's a Spirit to spirit, a tree of life, Christ in you frequency that you fine-tune and listen to it all the time.

OTHER BOOKS BY DON KEATHLEY

These titles can be found on Amazon

HELL'S ILLUSION

RELIGION BUSTERS

For more information about Don Keathley or to contact him please visit www.donkeathley.com

The Writer's Society is a hybrid self publishing company empowering authors to release books that reveal God's goodness to the world through a variety of self publishing services.

www.thewriterssociety.online

NOTES

NOTES

NOTES

NOTES

NOTES

Made in the USA
Coppell, TX
31 March 2025

47742587R10049